GEORGE FERRIS
WHAT A WHEEL

by Barbara Lowell
illustrated by Jerry Hoare and with photographs

Grosset & Dunlap
An Imprint of Penguin Group (USA) LLC

For Jim and Jeni—BL

GROSSET & DUNLAP
Published by the Penguin Group
Penguin Group (USA) LLC, 375 Hudson Street, New York, New York 10014, USA

USA | Canada | UK | Ireland | Australia | New Zealand | India | South Africa | China

penguin.com
A Penguin Random House Company

Photo credits: front cover: Special Collections Research Center, University of Chicago; back cover: (wheel images) Library of Congress, Prints and Photographs Division; page 1-32: (paper background) © Agata Kuczmińska/iStock/Getty Images; page 3: Library of Congress, Prints and Photographs Division; page 6: (street) Library of Congress, Prints and Photographs Division, (poster) © Chicago History Museum, (map) Library of Congress, Geography and Map Division; page 18: (trains) © Chicago History Museum, (engine) Cornell University Library; page 19: (air brake) Library of Congress, Prints and Photographs Division, (axle) © Chicago History Museum; page 22: © Chicago History Museum; page 23: (wheel) Special Collections Research Center, University of Chicago Library, (midway) Library of Congress, Prints and Photographs Division; page 26: (car) © Chicago History Museum, (wheel) Library of Congress, Prints and Photographs Division; page 29: (wheel) Library of Congress, Prints and Photographs Division, (midway) Wisconsin Historial Society, WHS-7384; page 30: (wheel) Wisconsin Historial Society, WHS-7386, (souvenir) The Newberry Library; page 31: (wheel) Special Collections Research Center, University of Chicago Library, (ticket) Special Collections Research Center, University of Chicago Library; page 32: Library of Congress, Geography and Map Division.

Library of Congress Cataloging-in-Publication Data is available.

ISBN 978-0-448-47925-5 (pbk)
ISBN 978-0-448-47926-2 (hc)

10 9 8 7 6 5 4 3 2 1
10 9 8 7 6 5 4 3 2 1

George Ferris was an engineer who had big ideas.
He turned his big ideas into bridges made of steel.
Bridges that crossed high over rivers.
Bridges that were strong and safe.
George made sure of that.

Before George ever imagined designing and building bridges, he lived with his family on a ranch in Nevada. A waterwheel nearby scooped up river water and spilled it into a trough for thirsty horses.

George would sit for hours and watch that wheel turn.

When he grew up, George remembered
the wheel.

The way it turned. The way it picked up
water. Everything about it.

He didn't know the waterwheel
would help him with his big
ideas. But it did.

By 1892, George was a respected engineer. He started and ran two engineering companies, one that designed and built bridges and one that tested steel that would be used in construction.

At a meeting of engineers in Chicago, George heard some exciting news. The World's Fair, a huge exhibition, would be held there the next year. Famous inventors, musicians, and artists would show off their creations. The inventor Thomas Edison would be there. So would Scott Joplin, a famous piano player. And people from over forty-six countries would visit the fair!

There would be lots to see and do. Including balloon rides.
An ostrich farm. And Buffalo Bill's Wild West Show.
But the people in charge wanted something new.
Something daring. Something they had never seen before.
George knew he was the person to create it.

At first, George didn't like any of his ideas.
Then the waterwheel popped into his head.

George grabbed some paper. He drew an
enormous wheel with cars on it for people
to ride in.

This was his biggest idea ever!

He showed lots of engineers his drawing. They shook their heads. They thought his design looked like a spiderweb—too fragile for anyone to ride.

But George liked his idea. He'd make it work. He'd make it strong and safe.

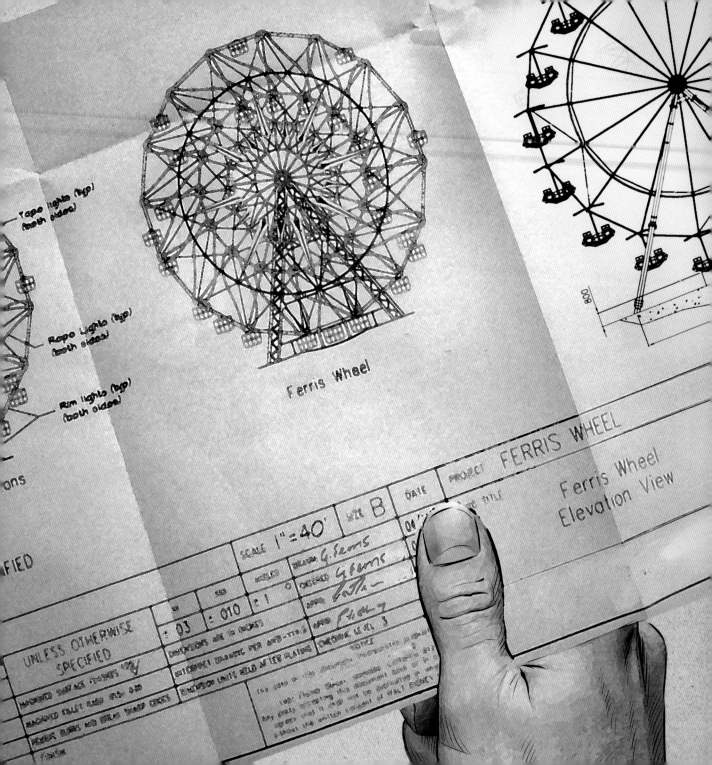

Tape lights (typ)
(both sides)

Rope lights (typ)
(both sides)

Rim lights (typ)
(both sides)

Ferris Wheel

800

					PROJECT	FERRIS WHEEL	

SCALE 1"=40' SIZE B DATE 04/

DRAWN G.Ferns

CHECKED Ferns

APPR

Ferris Wheel
Elevation View

UNLESS OTHERWISE SPECIFIED			

.03 .010 ± 1

George asked an engineering friend to help him.

They drew up a daring design—a giant 250-foot wheel made of strong yet lightweight steel. It looked like a bicycle wheel.

The thirty-six train-size cars were the best part. 2,160 people could ride the wheel at the same time!

No one had ever seen anything like it.

George raced to show the fair officials.

They reminded him that Chicago was nicknamed the Windy City for a reason. A thunderstorm could blow his wheel over. They told him his idea was too dangerous. Anyway, he'd have to pay to build his wheel.

George was disappointed, but he wasn't about to give up on his biggest idea ever. He'd convince them that his wheel would be safe—and he'd find the money to build it.

George needed a lot of money. The equivalent of millions of dollars today.

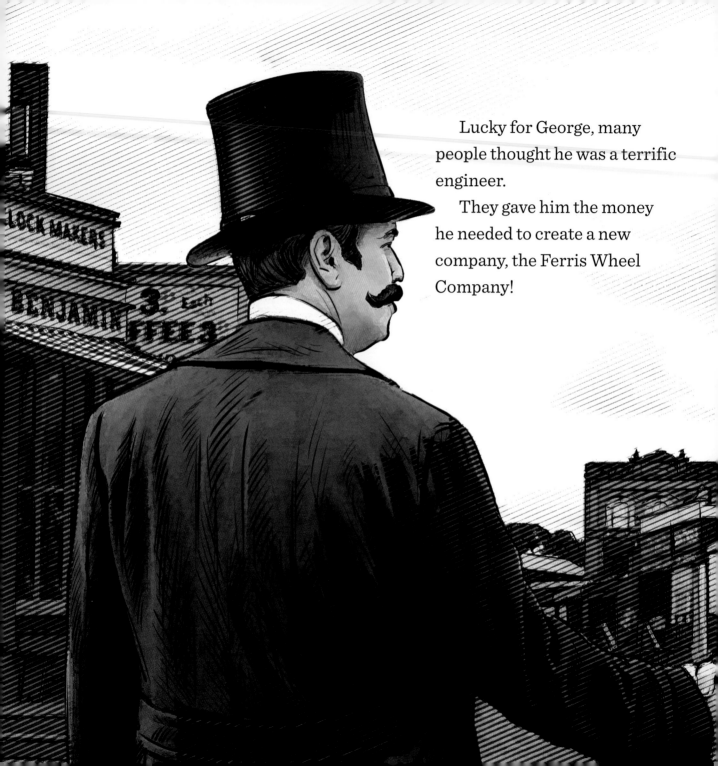

Lucky for George, many people thought he was a terrific engineer.

They gave him the money he needed to create a new company, the Ferris Wheel Company!

George reworked his plans and drawings a bit.

Now he had a solid plan and the money to build the wheel.

He dashed to find the fair officials.

They asked him lots of questions. And he had all the right answers.

Finally, they told him YES! But they wanted the wheel ready by opening day.

George was thrilled, but building a strong bridge took years. Could he build his wheel in less than five months?

He hoped so.

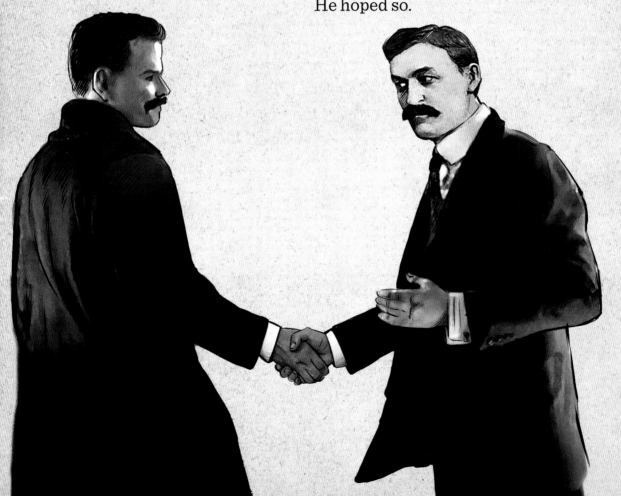

George ordered:

Steel parts that filled one hundred fifty freight train cars.

Three thousand electric lights.

A one-thousand-horsepower steam engine and an extra one in case the first broke down.

Air brakes to stop the wheel
in an instant.

And a ninety-thousand-pound
axle, the largest built at the time.

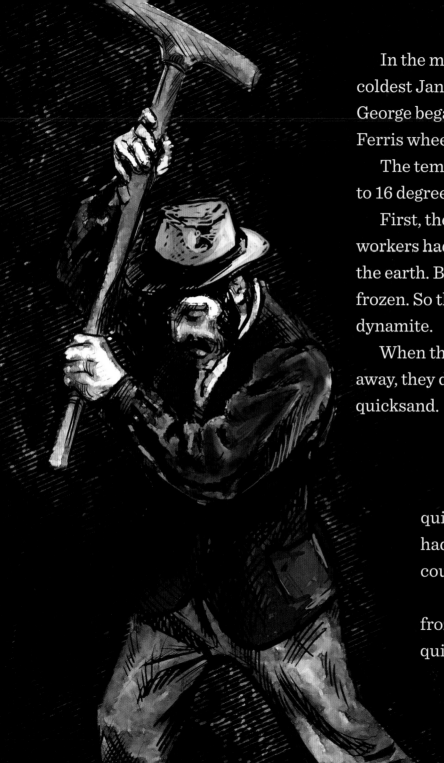

In the middle of one of the coldest Januarys in Chicago, George began work on the Ferris wheel.

The temperature plunged to 16 degrees below zero.

First, the construction workers had to dig deep into the earth. But the ground was frozen. So they blasted it with dynamite.

When the top layer blew away, they dug down and hit quicksand.

In Chicago? Yes! Frozen quicksand. All that quicksand had to be pumped out so they could reach the bedrock below.

They shot hot steam at the frozen ground and pumped the quicksand out.

Once the quicksand was out, the workers dug deeper into the earth. They drilled into the rock and pushed in steel bars.

They connected the bars to the legs of the two towers that would hold up the wheel.

They rushed to build the towers. Then swung the giant axle into place.

With opening day a month away, they raced to build the wheel.

Everyone worked hard and fast—but not fast enough.

On May 1, 1893, the fair opened. The Ferris wheel wasn't finished.

That didn't stop the workers. They continued the job tirelessly.

Finally...

…at the beginning of June, the Ferris wheel (minus the cars) soared above the fair.

It was time for a test run.

Everyone wondered: Would it really work? That is, everyone but George.

The boilers fired up. Steam pushed through the pipes and into the engine.
The brake holding the wheel tight was released and then—the Ferris wheel turned!
Excited construction workers leaped on.
People from all over the fair ran to watch.

The workers hung the first six cars.

With the extra weight, would the wheel still work? George had confidence. And Mrs. Ferris did, too.

She climbed into a car, ready for the wheel to turn.

At the top of the wheel—264 feet in the air—Mrs. Ferris jumped up on her chair and cheered!

The last cars were hung. The lights were connected. Now people packed into six lines waiting to ride George Ferris's wheel.

But first, George and Mrs. Ferris hopped into one car. A forty-piece marching band squeezed into another, and up, up, up they went.

The band played "America."

George rose higher and higher above the fair.

His biggest idea ever had worked. Just as he knew it would.

FERRIS WHEEL FACTS

- 1.5 million tickets were sold at the 1893 Chicago World's Fair.

- A ticket to ride the Ferris wheel cost fifty cents. Today, you would pay thirteen dollars to ride George's wheel.

- Each ride on the Ferris wheel lasted twenty minutes, with two revolutions. It took five minutes to ride from the bottom to the top to see a panoramic view of Chicago.

- If the Ferris wheel could be rolled out in a straight line, its 785-foot circumference would cover two NFL football fields, plus an extra fifty feet.

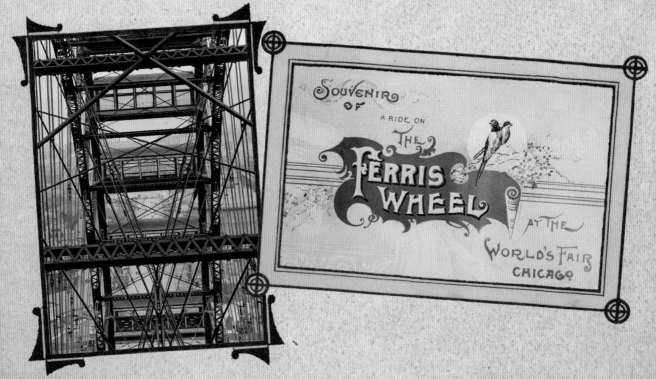

- The wheel weighed 1,520,996 pounds. The thirty-six cars together weighed 416,817 pounds. The 2,160 passengers weighed at least 216,000 pounds (if the average weight was one hundred pounds). The spokes supported over two million pounds!

- At the time the construction workers raised the axle, no one had ever lifted one that heavy or that high up before. They finished the job in only two hours.

- When Mrs. Ferris jumped up on her chair, she was especially brave. The glass for the windows hadn't been installed yet!

- On July 9, a fierce thunderstorm tested the Ferris wheel when it hit the fair with winds of 110 miles per hour. Passengers riding the wheel had to pull hard to keep the doors closed, but felt only a bit more vibration than normal.

- Teddy Roosevelt, Thomas Edison, Harry Houdini, Helen Keller, Annie Oakley, and Wilbur and Orville Wright attended the fair. Did they ride the Ferris wheel? No one is certain, but Chief Standing Bear wore a two-hundred-feather headdress when he took his turn.

- A star of the 1904 St. Louis World's Fair: the Ferris wheel!

- Many people believe that the inspiration for the Ferris wheel was the Cradlebaugh Bridge waterwheel near George Ferris's childhood home in Carson City, Nevada. Two other large wheels used the same tension principle that Ferris used for his wheel. Both were built in Michigan in the 1880s. One is the Burden wheel, a waterwheel sixty feet in diameter with twenty-two-foot-long buckets that operated near the college George Ferris attended in upstate New York.

- The Ferris wheel collapsed in 1906—not in a storm, but in a controlled dynamite explosion. Its parts were sold as salvage. Sadly, George Ferris had no say in the wheel's final outcome. He died ten years earlier at age thirty-seven of either typhoid fever or Bright's disease, a kidney condition.

- Taller observation wheels operate in the world today. The tallest, the Singapore Flyer, stands 541 feet high, nearly twice as tall as the Ferris wheel. The Flyer carries 784 passengers total, 1,376 less than George Ferris's wheel.

BIRD'S-EYE VIEW OF THE WORLD'S COLUMBIAN EXPOSITION, CHICAGO, 1893.